Pet Hamsters

Cecelia H. Brannon

Enslow Publishing
101 W. 23rd Street
Suite 240
New York, NY 10011
USA
enslow.com

Published in 2017 by Enslow Publishing, LLC.
101 W. 23rd Street, Suite 240, New York, NY 10011

Library of Congress Cataloging-in-Publication Data

Names: Brannon, Cecelia H., author.
Title: Pet hamsters / Cecelia H. Brannon.
Description: New York, NY : Enslow Publishing, 2017. | Series: All about pets | Audience: Age 6-up. | Audience: K to grade 3. | Includes   bibliographical references and index.
Identifiers: LCCN 2015045446| ISBN 9780766076013 (library bound) | ISBN 9780766076082 (pbk.) | ISBN 9780766075832 (6-pack)
Subjects: LCSH: Hamsters as pets--Juvenile literature.
Classification: LCC SF459.H3 B73 2017 | DDC 636.935/6--dc23
LC record available at http://lccn.loc.gov/2015045446

Printed in Malaysia

To Our Readers: We have done our best to make sure all website addresses in this book were active and appropriate when we went to press. However, the author and the publisher have no control over and assume no liability for the material available on those websites or on any websites they may link to. Any comments or suggestions can be sent by e-mail to customerservice@enslow.com.

Photos Credits: Cover, stock_shot/Shutterstock.com; p. 1 Yury Puzanov/Shutterstock.com; pp. 3 (left), 6; ultrapro/iStock/Thinkstock; pp. 3 (center), 20 iStock.com/AlexKalashnikov; pp. 3 (right), 10 Igor Podgorny/Shutterstock.com; pp. 4–5 Just_One_Pic/Shutterstock.com; pp. 8, 12 fantom_rd/Shutterstock.com; p. 14 Punyaphat Larpsomboon/Shutterstock.com; p. 16 LIUSHENGFILM/Shutterstock.com; p. 18 fotogigi85/Shutterstock.com; p. 22 2xSamara.com/Shutterstock.com.

Contents

Words to Know

cage

paw

pellet

Hamsters make great pets. They are friendly and love to play.

4

Hamsters live in a cage.
The cage must be cleaned
at least once a week.

A hamster runs on a wheel to exercise. This helps it stay healthy.

Hamsters eat seeds, nuts, and special food called pellets.

But hamsters eat fruit, too.
You can share a healthy
snack with your hamster!

A hamster has special pouches in its cheeks. This is where it keeps food when it is not chewing it.

A hamster drinks water from a special bottle in its cage. It needs fresh water every day.

A hamster likes to chew.
This helps it keep its teeth
clean, sharp, and short.

You do not have to bathe a hamster. It will clean itself by wiping its fur with its paws.

Hamsters are very soft. It is fun to hold your hamster. Your hamster will like it, too!

Read More

Heneghan, Judith. *Love Your Hamster*. New York: Windmill Books, 2013.

Hutmacher, Kimberly M. *I Want a Hamster*. North Mankato, MN: Capstone Press, 2012.

Websites

Easy Science for Kids
easyscienceforkids.com/all-about-hamsters/

National Geographic Kids
kids.nationalgeographic.com/explore/nature/wild-hamsters/

Index

Guided Reading Level: B
Guided Reading Leveling System is based on the guidelines recommended by Fountas and Pinnell.

Word Count: 150